JOHNSON MEDIA CENTER

Ralph M. T. Johnson School
Bethel Educational Park
Whittlesey Drive
Bethel, Connecticut 06801

Video Game Designer

Walter Oleksy

JOHNSON MEDIA CENTER

the rosen publishing group's
rosen central
new york

Published in 2000 by The Rosen Publishing Group, Inc.
29 East 21st Street, New York, NY 10010

Copyright ©2000 by The Rosen Publishing Group, Inc.

First Edition

All rights reserved. No part of this book may be reproduced in any form without permission in writing from the publisher, except by a reviewer.

Library of Congress Cataloging-in-Publication Data

Oleksy, Walter.
   Video game designer / Oleksy
      p. cm. — (CoolCareers.Com)
   Includes bibliographical references.
   Summary: Discusses what education and skills are needed to become a video game designer and profiles several successful game designers.
   ISBN 0-8239-3117-X (lib. bdg.)
   1. Computer games—Programming—Vocational Guidance Juvenile literature. 2. Video games—Design—Vocational guidance. [1. Video games—Design—Vocational guidance. 2. Vocational guidance. 3. Occupations.] I. Title. II. Series.
QA76.76.C672044   2000
794.8' 151—dc21   99-38343
                                                              CIP

Manufactured in the United States of America

CONTENTS

ABOUT THIS BOOK

Technology is changing all the time. Just a few years ago, hardly anyone who wasn't a hardcore technogeek had heard of the Internet or the World Wide Web. Computers and modems were way slower and less powerful. If you said "dot com," no one would have any idea what you meant. Hard to imagine, isn't it?

It is also hard to imagine how much more change and growth is possible in the world of technology. People who work in the field are busy imagining, planning, and working toward the future, but even they can't be sure how computers and the Internet will look and function by the time you are ready to start your career. This book is intended to give you an idea of what is out there now so that you can think about what interests you and how to find out more about it.

One thing is clear: Computer-related occupations will continue to increase in number and variety. The demand for qualified workers in these extremely cool fields is increasing all the time. So if you want to get a head start on the competition, or if you just like to fool around with computers, read on!

chapter one

A CAREER IN VIDEO GAMES?

Do you like to spend your time after school with an electronic game player, or with a CD-ROM game disk in your home computer? Do you like to pretend that you're the ex-soldier Cloud, trying to save the planet from destruction by the evil corporation Shinra in *Final Fantasy VII*? Maybe action's your thing, and you prefer playing *Shadow Warrior*, *Tomb Raider*, or *Blade Runner*. How

Do you like playing video games in your free time?

about sports? When you're not playing Little League at the community park, do you like to belt one out of the virtual ballpark in an interactive baseball video game like *High Heat*?

If you like to play video games, maybe you've wondered about a career as a video game designer. That's not as unrealistic a goal as you might think. Thousands of people make their living creating video games. They love it, and they make very good money doing it too. Some experienced video game designers can make more than $100,000 a year. If you have a lively imagination and some talent in design or writing, a career as a video game designer may be in your future.

In this book, you'll learn what video game designers do and how they do it. You'll learn about the present and future of video game design. You'll also meet some of the very creative and talented people who earn high salaries while enjoying this exciting career. Then you can decide if a cool career as a video game designer is for you.

chapter two

WHAT IS A VIDEO GAME DESIGNER?

Video game designers or developers conceive the overall idea of a video game. They work out its plot, its characters, its action sequences, and the general rules of play. These details are known as the game's concept. They then work to pilot that concept all the way through to the actual production of the game. It is fair to say, then, that the video game designer is the "author" of the game, the person whose basic idea shapes the story and the action of the game.

The video game designer begins with a description of the game, a "script" written out much as one would write a short story. It describes the goals of the game, how it should be played, and the different levels of play. The animated, or moving, characters, called sprites, are described as well. The game designer makes sketches and

gathers background artwork to support this script. All of this material comprises the initial "documentation" of the game and describes not how the game works from a technical viewpoint, but how it is played and how it will look. This documentation is presented to the programmers and animators and guides them as they work on various aspects of the game.

After this stage, just how much a designer may be involved in further development of the game depends upon his or her skills. The design of the game still has to be refined, the program must be written, the characters have to be animated, the graphic elements must be prepared, and the sound effects need to be added. Then the whole game must be tested and perfected before marketing. In testing, the game not only has to work, but it has to be easy and fun to play.

Some video games are created by just one very talented person. Besides having strong writing and artistic skills, such individuals are excellent computer programmers. Most important of all, they have a vivid imagination. Often, however, it can take more than 200 talented and imaginative people to design, produce, and market a successful video game, according to the Computer Game Developers Conference. Most games require the skills of at least twenty people just to create the computer program and artwork. The remaining 180 people may be involved in publishing and marketing the game.

Video game designers are paid well for their work. They can earn upwards of $85,000 a year and may also receive royalties. Royalties are a percentage of all sales income paid to the designer for his or her special contribution in designing the game. Royalties can double or triple a designer's total earnings. If the video game designer does not have all the skills required to design the game, he or she will work with a team. Let's look at some of the talented people who might make up this team.

The Programmer ▶▶▶▶▶▶▶▶▶▶

Programmers take the concepts that designers create and turn these ideas into games by writing the coded instructions, or programs that tell the computer what to do. These people must translate animated characters, screen movements, and changing graphic displays into lines of computer code that are read in the proper sequence. Programmers earn $45,000 or more a year. Senior programmers earn over $55,000 a year. Without programmers, there would be no computer games. They must have a fast computer with a lot of memory, a modem and an Internet connection, a scanner, and a color printer.

Programmers need creative problem-solving skills. They must be able to take a complex series of actions and break them down into simple instructions that a computer can process one at a time. They must know how to create the illusion that many actions are taking place at once, and they have to anticipate how each action of the player will change the outcome of the game. They must also know at least some computer programming languages. Visual Basic is the world's most popular programming language, but it is relatively slow compared to Visual C++, which is the preferred computer language for game programming. Many games are written in programs such as BASIC, Pascal, and Delphi.

To write the graphics for a video game, it is very important for a programmer to have a knowledge of

assembly language. Assembly language works "below" the more user-friendly programming languages. A commercial graphics library such as Fastgraph can help you master assembly language. A compiler is another necessary tool of game programming. Compilers translate programming languages into codes that your computer can understand. The Watcom C/C++ compiler for Windows is a popular one.

Programmers must have the ability to think logically. Programmers must break down all the complicated actions required by the game designers into logical steps that the computer can execute. Computers are very fast, but they process only one instruction at a time, in the order that they are found in the written program. If the programmer doesn't put the instructions in the proper order, the program may not work correctly. The program also may "crash," and then your computer will stop working altogether. If this sounds very complicated, it doesn't have to be. You can learn computer and game programming from a game called *Logiblocs*. Using various electronic "building blocks," *Logiblocs* makes it far less complicated, and fun, to learn the processes involved in programming.

These programming aids can be very helpful, and they are useful for experimenting with your first few video games. In the long run, however, it is probably better not to depend on shortcuts in mastering programming.

Programming is a fascinating field that will teach you a great deal about how computers work. It will teach problem-solving skills, and it will give you the inside track on how to work closely with programmers as a video game designer.

Artists

Also called animators, artists produce the artwork for a game program and scan it into their computers. They need to be familiar with the latest advances in computer graphics and simulation techniques (methods of imitating real objects and real movements on the computer screen). A strong background in 3-D computer design and animation is essential.

Original artwork or CD-ROM stock illustrations ("clip art") are scanned into a computer to illustrate a game. A computer painting or drawing program can also be used to create the artwork. So can a rendering program, which is even better. Game animators are often paid a set fee for an entire project, ranging from $30,000 to $50,000, rather than receiving a weekly or monthly salary.

Musicians ▶▶▶▶▶▶▶▶▶

Musicians create the music and sound effects for the game. Salaries for video game musicians vary widely. Post-production engineers, digital remastering engineers, and MIDI engineers (all of whom work to transform music and sound into digital files that computers  can read) earn between $40,000 and $70,000 a year. Starting salaries are much lower. Many in this field are freelancers who are paid by the job rather than full-time salaried employees.

Testers ▶▶▶▶▶▶▶▶▶

Beta testers test a game for technical problems (bugs). Play testers test for how well the game plays (how much fun it is and how it challenges the players). Salaries average $30,000 to $50,000 a year. The role of testers is very important. The testing stage is when a game designer learns if all of his or her clever ideas actually work or if they only confuse or bore the player. Most games are changed before they go on the market as a result of this trial-and error process. Testing is a critical stage for everyone involved. If the game doesn't work, that's one problem. But if the game is simply dull, if the action is too difficult to control, or if bugs in the program allow the player to break the rules, the designer faces serious problems.

Testers look for all kinds of bugs. Major bugs will cause a crash. The computer will shut down or the on-screen action will freeze. But other problems are less obvious and require skill and experience to evaluate. Is there something awkward, unrealistic, or too fast or too slow about the way the animated characters or the backgrounds move? Is there something confusing about the design or the artwork? Testers might also suggest improvements to make the game more interesting or more playable.

The Producer ▶▶▶▶▶▶▶▶▶▶

The producer is the person who oversees development of the game and makes sure that all the elements are in place. He or she coordinates the work of everyone else and ensures that everyone is assigned the proper work, all deadlines are met, and costs stay under control. Salaries average over $50,000 a year.

The producer is the project manager. In the on-line game developer's magazine *Gamasutra* (http://www.gamasutra.com),

Roger Pedersen wrote that "This person is a diplomat, a politician, a trouble-shooter, a force needed to produce the product."

The Publisher ▶▶▶▶▶▶▶▶▶

Video games are sold to the public either by established game companies, by publishers, or by independent businesspeople who sell the games themselves. Publishers often earn high salaries, from $75,000 to over $1 million a year.

TYPES OF VIDEO GAMES ▶▶▶▶▶▶▶▶

There are several kinds of computer games, each requiring special skills to create. Adventure games, like *Monkey Island* and *Myst*, have a lot of action and graphics. The player usually has to solve a mystery or puzzle. Side scrollers are games like *Super Mario Brothers* or *Commander Keen*, in which the background scrolls, or slides, behind the animated characters. Twitch games, like *Doom* or *Quake*, are games in which players shoot at objects. These require good eye-to-hand coordination. There are role-playing games and arcade games as well.

HOW TO DESIGN A VIDEO GAME

When he was only eight years old and in second grade, a Minnesota boy named Scott Schubert interviewed his classmates for an independent study project he called "All About

Video Games." In it he gives one of the simplest and best descriptions of what goes into designing a video game:

- 💾 Get the idea for the game.
- 💾 Design what will happen and how the characters will look.
- 💾 Plan all the levels for the game, and design the scenery for every level.
- 💾 Draw the characters and the scenery.
- 💾 Draw a storyboard for what happens when.
- 💾 Write the script for the game.
- 💾 Make the animation.
- 💾 Make the game program, putting together the drawings, animation, and action.
- 💾 Write the music.
- 💾 Add the music and sounds to the game.
- 💾 Test the game for problems.
- 💾 Fix the problems.
- 💾 Manufacture the game.

The newest video game Scott has designed is a fantasy called *Medieval.* "You go on a quest to find King Arthur and Excalibur and bring them back to Camelot," says Scott, who is now twelve years old. He made the game using HyperStudio. You can play it if you have a Macintosh computer with a

HyperStudio 3.0 player. To play *Medieval*, go to Scott's Web site at *http://www.1.minn.net/~schubert/VGall/html*. Scott, who is now 12 years old, is interviewed in chapter 4 along with other video game designers.

LET TECHNOLOGY DO THE WORK

Designing a video game may not be an easy task, but special computer software programs can be helpful aids. Many young people are creating their own interactive video games by using them.

HyperStudio is one example. This software is a multimedia tool for creating games and other interactive projects. It helps users to create text, sound, graphics, and video on a disk, CD-ROM, or over the Internet.

Rocket Science Games, a video game design company in Redwood City, California, also markets software to help in creating video games. Their product, called Game Science, is made up of two tools called Game Composer and Game Compiler. Game Composer creates a working blueprint of a video game. Even beginners who don't know computer programming languages can put their ideas into game form. Once a game is completed, Game Compiler allows the user to produce the game for various systems such as Sega CD or PC CD-ROM. Rocket Science's best-selling video games are *Rocket Jockey*, *The Space Bar*, and *Obsidian*.

Many video game designers, writers, and artists work for major companies such as Sony PlayStation, Atari, and Mattel. Others work independently as part of a team of people who create and market their own games.

New video games are always in demand because most games are sold in stores for only six months at most, and then room is made on the shelves for new ones. Exceptions are blockbuster games such as Myst and Doom. Many less famous but low-priced video games that cost from $6 to $15 are available in stores much longer than the more expensive ones. Video games can take from eight months to two years to program and bring to market. Many games sell upwards of 25,000 copies.

chapter three

THE FUTURE FOR VIDEO GAME DESIGNERS

Video games are among the newest of electronic entertainments. Since they were introduced in 1972, they have grown into an exciting multibillion-dollar industry. Video game fans spent a whopping $7 billion buying video games and players in 1998, according to the Electronic Industries Association. That was about as much as movie theater owners took in at their box offices.

The video game industry's future seems assured. Millions of kids play video games, and so do a growing number of adults. Many adults enjoy playing sports video games. Others like games based upon historical events. One example is the *Battle of Gettysburg*,

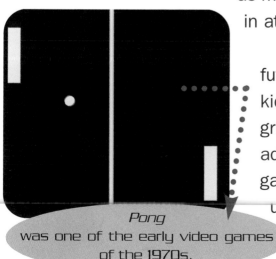

Pong was one of the early video games of the 1970s.

in which players interact with history by changing the outcome of this famous Civil War battle.

Industry analysts predict an even healthier future for video games as new technology comes into play. This technology will include digital and satellite television, as well as superfast fiber-optic cable modems for on-line play. We can also expect to see more powerful chips that can produce faster and smoother action, more lifelike characters, and more realistic backgrounds. It was really the revolution in chip speed and increased memory that made possible the complicated, animated, fast-moving games that dominate the video game market today.

Electronic industry leaders predict that video games will be with us far into the twenty-first century. Regulations may be passed to govern their violent content, but all over the world, video games are too big a part of popular culture to go away.

CAREER OPPORTUNITIES ▶▶▶▶▶▶▶▶

Video game companies and freelance game designers are continually competing with each other by introducing new games and players as technology in the field advances. If you search the Internet for video game companies, you will find that they are always looking for new talent. They need game designers, programmers, and artists in order to keep ahead of the competition. Many companies advertise on-line to find skilled employees. Classified ads in major national newspapers are another good place to look for such jobs, and in many cases beginning salaries are quite generous.

In the spring of 1999, Capcom Digital Studios (part of Capcom USA) in Sunnyvale, California, announced that it was moving heavily in the direction of 3-D games. The company's Web site indicated that it was in need of experienced 3-D programmers "with a passion for playing and creating top-quality games." Capcom needed 3-D artists as well.

Sega of America, another major video game company, has also advertised on-line for game talent. It was in need of

game designers, artist-animators, on-line producers, associate producers, game programmers, and senior game programmers. The extra talent was needed as Sega launched Dreamcast, its next-generation video game console, for autumn of 1999. The new game player doubles as a CD player and has an Internet interface so that gamers can go directly on-line to the World Wide Web.

A Sega spokesman said that the player's 128-bit processor and 200-megahertz (MHz) computer chip makes it "the most powerful video game console ever created." He said that it is fifteen times more powerful than Sony's PlayStation and ten times faster than Nintendo 64. It is the first game system to include a 56K modem, allowing gamers to play on-line as well as browse the Web.

Sony, not to be left in the dust of virtual reality games, introduced its new PlayStation II. Also powered by a 128-bit processor running at 300 MHz, PlayStation II is many times more powerful than earlier players. This allows for a big upgrade in graphics quality, 3-D imagery, and video capability.

GIRLS AT THE CONTROLS ▶▶▶▶▶▶▶▶▶▶

The video game industry is now paying more attention to female gamers. More video game designers, especially

Lara Croft of Tomb Raider.

women, are being sought to supply the increasing demand from girls and women who play video games. The trend to attract more women to video games began in 1998 when Purple Moon's girls' game *Rockett's World* reached $5 million in sales. Mattel bought the company and a year later launched the legendary Barbie Doll into her own CD-ROM girls' game, Barbie. Mattel's goal was "to introduce every girl in the country" to its computer game.

Competing with Mattel for the girls' video game market is Girl Games, Inc., with its own popular game *Teen Digital Diva*. Almost as real to many players is the fictitious Lara Croft, who is called the cyberqueen of video games. The animated action heroine has sold millions of dollars in game software. She has also inspired lines of comic books, dolls, and clothing; more than 100 fan sites on the Internet; and even a movie.

POP MUSIC AND SPORTS GO GAMING ▶▶▶▶▶▶▶▶▶▶

Another new trend in video games is more use of music from popular CDs or from original tracks composed by major recording artists. One example is the driving game *Rollcage* from the British game company Psygnosis. This action game involving sports cars comes with music from the rap star Fatboy Slim's chart-soaring CD *You've Come a Long Way Baby.*

Sports star power also has been added to top-selling video games. For example, Michael Jordan appeared as a character in the video game spin-off of his hit movie *Space Jam.* This basketball video game from PlayStation sold for only $10 and became a top-selling game in 1999.

Besides real-life sports figures and other celebrities, animated characters from movies and television series are

also becoming video game stars. These include the character Cartman from the animated *South Park* television series, who stars in a video game for Nintendo 64 and PC formats. Flick, the popular animated ant from the hit movie *A Bug's Life,* starred in a video game from Sony PlayStation.

NOT JUST FOR KIDS ANYMORE

Perhaps the biggest future trend for video gaming is the industry's effort to attract more grown-ups to the games. Top adult video games of 1999 included *The Legend of Zelda: Ocarina of Time* ($70), an adventure game aimed at the whole family. Adults also went for the James Bond-inspired game *Goldeneye 007* ($40) and the 3-D game *Deer Hunter II* ($20). Adults especially like to play video games on-line. Playing a game to relax at night after work can be fun for an adult, and by going on-line, you can play with other people. On the Internet, gamers can compete with other players in a distant city or country. CD-ROM strategy games such as *StarCraft* or the science game *Half-Life* are best played with another person.

VIOLENCE: A CAUTIONARY NOTE

Excessive violence in films, on television, and in video games is now on the minds of parents, teachers, politicians, and concerned individuals. There is a fear that such violence will encourage young people to commit violent acts in the real world, or at the very least become indifferent toward real violence.

If you choose a career as a video game designer, this issue should be of concern to you. Of course, it may be hard or boring to design an action video game in which no aliens are blasted away, no evil conquerors are slain, and no villains meet their just and painful end. All the same, it's something you should be thinking about as you design your games. Is all that blood and gore really necessary to enjoy the game? Do any of the scenarios in your game show abusive behavior toward women, or toward others? Are there not other ways to make your game interesting and fun to play? Self-restraint on the part of video game designers could help to prevent politicians from attempting to regulate the industry.

GAME DESIGNER JOBS TODAY AND TOMORROW ►►►►►►►►►

Game companies all over the world are hiring young men and women with experience in all aspects of video game design. Many of these companies consider the game designer to be the most important member of their business.

The video game industry has high expectations for the future as the boundaries blur between gaming machines, television, Hollywood films, and computers. Many of the most successful video games released today are spin-offs based on story lines and characters from movies and television programs. This will mean more career opportunities for those talented enough to design the games.

Men and women who work as video game designers have special skills in graphic arts and computer programming. All of them are highly creative, imaginative people. Here are the stories of several successful people who want to share their knowledge and experience with others who might want to become video game designers.

chapter four

PEOPLE WHO DESIGN VIDEO GAMES

SHIGERU MIYAMOTO ▶▶▶▶▶▶▶▶▶

One of the most successful designers of video games is Shigeru Miyamoto, who works at Nintendo's headquarters in Tokyo, Japan. The creator of over sixty games in his twenty-two years with Nintendo, he was the idea man behind the pioneering games *Donkey Kong* and *Super Mario Brothers*. He also created the *Legend of Zelda* CD-ROM series that sold more than 1.6 million copies when it was first introduced in 1997.

"I've always loved to draw cartoon characters," says Miyamoto. "That led me to create video games."

Miyamoto got his degree in industrial design from a college in Tokyo. In 1977 he was hired as Nintendo's first staff artist. He created the *Donkey Kong* arcade game four years later. Then he designed the spin-off video game as well as the first *Super Mario* game. The adventures of the Italian plumber with the droopy mustache became so popular that the game has earned Nintendo over $5 billion.

Since Miyamoto works for Nintendo, he receives no royalties from the games he designs, but he makes a very good salary. He and his wife live modestly in Kyoto and have a thirteen-year-old son and an eleven-year-old daughter. Miyamoto laughs as he says of his children, "They play video games but are not big fans of games. They are probably the only kids whose father plays video games better than they do."

DIANA GRUBER►►►►►►►►►

Diana Gruber, a freelance game designer in Las Vegas, Nevada, has been creating computer games since 1987. Her games are marketed by her husband's company, Ted Gruber Software. He is the author of Fastgraph, a computer software program that helps users add graphics to games.

"I am often asked, 'How can I learn to be a game designer?'" Diana Gruber says, "My answer is that unless you are lucky enough to be a student in a place where they offer good classes on the subject, you will need to teach yourself. The best way to do this is by collecting game information and then studying it. Use what you have learned to write game programs. The best sources of game information I know are Web sites and books."

EVAN MARGOLIN▶▶▶▶▶▶▶▶▶

Evan Margolin has been an avid video and arcade game player since he was a boy. He became a lawyer, then switched careers three years ago to work at his real love—games. He became a game designer for Cyclone Studios in San Mateo, California, and offers this advice on a career as a game designer:

"Most important is the ability to place yourself in the player's mind. As a designer, you have to be able to imagine how the game is played. You must see it from the eyes of the player. You have to plan out and script the overall game from the eyes of the person who will experience it.

"To be a designer, it really helps to have a solid and far-reaching gaming background. Know what has worked or failed in the past. Understanding why helps you avoid making the same mistakes.

"The single most important quality in such a demanding business is a tireless desire and drive to succeed. Although desire does not guarantee your success, it makes it far more likely."

WILLIAM ANDERSON ▶▶▶▶▶▶▶▶▷

A video game designer for eighteen years, William Anderson is now senior game designer at Capcom USA, a subsidiary of Sega Enterprises in San Francisco, California. The company has forty game designers, artists, and programmers on staff creating new games. Recent products include three popular action series, *Mega Man*, *Night Warrior*, and *Street Fighter*.

Anderson talks about his work and offers advice to those wanting to become video game designers: "The work of a game designer can vary. Each company has its own definition of what it wants from a game designer. The main thing is to be able to write a good story and tell how the game is to be played. Be able to describe what makes it challenging and unique.

"When I started in this business, one person was expected to do everything in designing a game. Now a team of eight to twenty-five people, all with different skills, will work together to create a game."

Anderson got his first job as a game designer by creating a sample game, and he recommends that beginners do the same. "It took about four months," Anderson recalls. "I wrote the story in a three-ring notebook. I explained how the game was to be played and how all the elements fit together. It covered about 250 pages including documents and diagrams.

"I sent it to a game company, hoping to get a programming job. But at the time, they needed a designer, not a programmer. They liked my sample work, and I got the job as a designer. I then worked on several popular new video games such as *Cool Spot*, *Aladdin,* and *Jungle Book*."

Anderson advises young people aspiring to become game designers, "Take a writing course, especially dramatic or action writing. Learn basic computer programming and computer art.

"This will give you a foundation for working with programmers and artists. You have to be able to communicate your ideas to them. Also, take technical courses such as flowcharting, diagram design, and mechanical drawing. The more skills you have, the better."

Anderson also says that it is important to play a lot of games. "Study them as you play. Notice the details. How many moves does it take to play the game? What buttons on the controls do what, and for how long? How many environments or levels are involved? How many bad guys are there in the game? What do they do and in what sequence? Knowing all this about a game will teach you to be a successful game designer."

chapter five

LEARNING MORE ABOUT GAME DESIGN

A PRETEEN GAME DESIGNER

Scott Schubert, a twelve-year-old student in the fifth grade in Minnesota, has already designed several video games, though they are not commercially available. "Two years ago I created a game called

Quest for Food," says Scott. "I made it on my Macintosh computer with the game-maker software HyperStudio. I won a blue ribbon for it at the Minnesota State Fair."

Scott created his fantasy game *Medieval* as part of a special programming class at his school.

"I made it using StoryMaker for Mac," he says. "It's an interactive game that required scripting and has animation features."

Scott likes video games that are full of action. His favorite is *Final Fantasy VII*. His ambition is to become a professional game designer. "I want to be a game designer because I like making the things I imagine come to life," says Scott. "Video games are a whole different world where anything can happen. It's fun to be someone else in a new situation for a while just by powering up. In games, I visit places you can't drive or fly to."

Scott finds educational benefits in video game playing. "Puzzle and strategy video games are helpful because I have to think about how to solve them, just like in school. And games are a great way to relax after school."

If you're interested in a career as a video game designer, maybe you can do what Scott did. Try designing your own game with Hyperstudio or some other game-making software.

AMATEUR DESIGNERS ▶▶▶▶▶▶▶▶▷

Many popular games are designed by people who are not employees of game companies but who design them simply as a hobby. These games are often available as "shareware." Rather than being marketed through a large corporation,

shareware is available for down-
loading from the Web sites of
smaller companies, individ-
ual programmers, and
game enthusiasts. People
offering shareware usu-
ally ask for a small fee or
ask that you use the game
only for a certain amount of
time before either discarding it or
paying for it. Many of these games are

just as complex and exciting as commercial products, and you
should look for them on the Web.

Video game designers all agree: play games and analyze
them. This process will give you the knowledge and experience you need to become a game designer. To be successful,
the games you design must appeal to a large number of
gamers, and must possess the kind of story lines, actions,
and artwork that make people want to play the game. By
studying existing video games, you learn what works, what
doesn't work, and what is popular.

Play all types of video games—educational ones as well as
action games. While playing a video game, pay attention to how
it is constructed. Study the graphics and the way the game is
played. Take notes to study how the game was programmed.

As you study other games, you'll come to understand some of the basic principles of game design. You must begin with a good story idea. You must create an interesting main character. The various levels of the game have to be planned out in advance. You must learn to program efficiently to save disk space. And the key strokes that control the action of the game need to be simple and easy to use. You can learn from the mistakes of others.

The Game Developer's Newsletter is available at *http://igdn.org.* Among other things, it lists upcoming conferences of game developers and designers. Some are held in exciting locations like London and Tokyo. But the Game Developer's Conference (GDC) itself sponsors a series of GDC RoadTrips, one day conventions in various U.S. cities. In 1999, the schedule included meetings in Boston, Chicago, Raleigh, Los Angeles, Salt Lake City, Austin, Marin, and Seattle. These are excellent places to meet other designers. The GDC also sponsors an annual Independent Games Festival. Find out more at *http://www.indie-games.com.* A group called Xtreme Games LLC, which focuses on non-commercial game development, holds an annual conference called

ARMAGEDDON. Find out about their next meeting at *http://www.xgames3d.com/armmain.htm.*

Try to meet video game designers. You'll find them at game trade shows and conferences. To learn where and when they may be in your town or city, go on-line to the Web site of the Computer Game Developer's Conference at *http://www.gdconf.com.* This organization also offers support and news to video game designers and developers.

Read books and magazines about video games and their design. Other books in the CoolCareers.Com series by the Rosen Publishing Group offer more information on subjects related to video game design. Additional books, as well as magazines about game designing and the video game industry, are listed in the back of this book.

Take classes at school that will teach you more about computers, programming, scanners, and the Internet. A great deal can be learned about video game design and careers in the field by visiting these other World Wide Web sites:

💾 http://www.igdn.org

The Web site of the International Game Developers Network, a nonprofit organization for game developers to share problems and solutions of game designing and news about their industry.

⊟ http://www.vaga.flame.org/developer

A vast on-line source of information on video game designing. At this site, be sure to go to Ben Sawyer's The Getting Started Guide to Game Development. It offers a wide range of information on game design.

For those who love to play video games, becoming a video game designer is a dream job. It is an exciting, creative, and rewarding career in an industry that has a very healthy future. Be sure to look in the For Further Information section for books and magazines about video game design. Here are a number of online resources that may be helpful:

Online Magazines ▶▶▶▶▶▶▶▶▶▶▶

GameFan Online: http://www.gamefan.com

Game Players: http://www.gameplayers.com

GamePro Online: http://www.gamepro.com

GameStation Online Magazine:
http://www.mds.mdh.se/~eko93pjn

WORDS.COM

animation   Techniques for creating moving characters and objects onscreen.

application   Another word for a program.

assembly language   The symbolic or mathematical code that can be read directly by your computer. Programming languages, which may employ "user-friendly" English words, are translated into machine-readable code by assembler software.

bugs   Programming mistakes that prevent a computer program from operating properly. In "beta testing," programmers run newly developed software and search for and correct mistakes, a process known as debugging.

CD-ROM   A "read-only memory" compact disk whose data is read by a laser.

compiler   Like assembler software, a compiler

program can translate "high-level" programming languages into machine-readable codes.

computer graphics   Computer-generated art and illustrations.

documentation   All of the notes, documents, outlines, and instructions created in the development of a piece of software that explain how that software was produced and what it is supposed to do.

fiber optics   Cables made from bundles of fine glass strands that transmit information along a beam of light.

freelance   To work independently under contract for someone, as opposed to being a salaried employee of a company.

memory   The amount of random access memory, not hard drive disk space, that a computer has. It is measured in megabytes, and the more memory a computer has, the faster it will operate.

MIDI (Musical Instrument Digital Interface)   An electronic file format that stores sounds in digital form.

modem   A computer accessory that translates data into tones sent over telephone lines.

multimedia   The combination of sound, pictures, animation, and text in one computer application.

on-line   Connecting to other computers through telephone lines using a modem.

producer   Someone who coordinates and supervises a

game's development.

programmer Someone who writes the coded instructions for a piece of software such as a video game.

publisher Someone who markets games.

royalties A method of payment based upon a percentage of sales. For example, a game designer might earn 5 percent of all income earned from the sale of his or her game.

scanner A computer accessory that "reads" images into a computer so that they can be used in a computer application.

simulation A multimedia application designed to look like a real-life environment.

stock illustrations Illustrations provided by a commercial photo archive, as opposed to original illustrations prepared for a specific project.

storyboard A set of drawings that show events in the sequence they are supposed to occur.

virtual Something that appears to be real but which is really a computer simulation.

3-D game A game with three-dimensional artwork.

RESOURCES.COM

Become a Video Game Developer
An On-line Book by Diana Gruber
http://www.makegames.com

Capcom Digital Studios
http://www.capcom.com

Fastgraph
http://www.fastgraph.com

Hyperstudio
http://www.hyperstudio.com

Logiblocs
http://www.logiblocs.com

Mattel
 http://www.girlgames.com

Sega
http://www.coga.com

Sony
http://www.sony.com

Storymaker
http://www.storymaker.com

Family Games!
http://familygames.com/index.html

Virtual Search
http://www.vsearch.com/designers

BOOKS.COM

Books

Dunne, Alex, Ben Sawyer, and Tor Berg. *Game Developer's Marketplace*. Scottsdale, AZ: Coriolis Group, 1998.

Gruber, Diana. *Action Arcade Adventure Set.* Las Vegas, NV: Fastgraph, 1997.

———.*Become a Video Game Developer.* Las Vegas, NV: Fastgraph, 1997. An on-line edition is available at http://www.makegames.com.

LaMothe, Andre. *Windows Game Programming for Dummies.* Foster City, CA: IDG Books Worldwide, 1998.

Lund, Bill. *A Career as a Video Game Designer.* Minneapolis,
MN: Capstone Press, 1998.

Print Magazines and Their Web Sites

Computer Games Strategy Plus:
http://www.cdmag.com

Computer Gaming World:
http://www.zdnet.com/gaming

Electronic Game Monthly:
http://www1.zdnet.com/zdsubs/egm/gamespot/aba

GamePro Magazine:
http://www.gamepro.com

Gamesmania:
http://www.gamesmania.com

PC Gamer:
http://www.pcgamer.com

PC Games:
http://www.pcgamesmag.com

INDEX

CREDITS

About the Author

Walter Oleksy is a freelance writer who has written several books on computer careers. He has also written biographies of Christopher Reeve, Princess Diana, and James Dean, as well as a new book on the Phillipines. His next biography will be about Leonardo DiCaprio. He lives in a suburb of Chicago with his dog Max.

Photo Credits

Cover by Shalhevet Moshe; pp. 15, 6, 9, 12, 25,35 © Uniphoto; pp. 8 © FPG; pp. 14 © Laura Croft art courtesy of EIDOS Interactive; pp. 23 © Evrett; pp. 24 © Thaddeus Harden; pp. 32 © Nancy Schubert; pp. 33, 36 © SuperStock.